S0-AAD-026

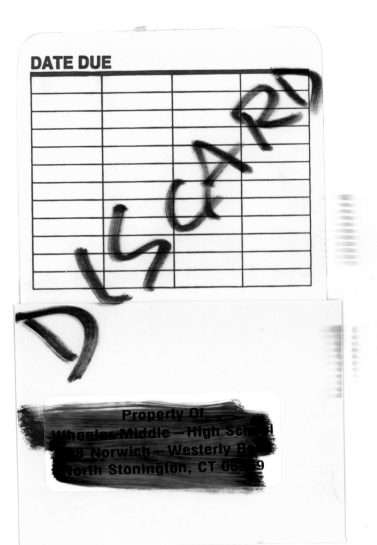

DATE DUE

DISCARD

Property Of
Wheeler Middle – High School
8 Norwich – Westerly Road
North Stonington, CT 06359

CAREERS IN
CRIMINAL
JUSTICE™

CAREERS IN THE
COURT
SYSTEM

Tamra B. Orr

ROSEN
PUBLISHING®

New York

Published in 2010 by The Rosen Publishing Group, Inc.
29 East 21st Street, New York, NY 10010

Copyright © 2010 by The Rosen Publishing Group, Inc.

First Edition

All rights reserved. No part of this book may be reproduced in any form without permission in writing from the publisher, except by a reviewer.

Library of Congress Cataloging-in-Publication Data

Orr, Tamra.
Careers in the court system / Tamra B. Orr.
    p. cm.—(Careers in criminal justice)
Includes bibliographical references and index.
ISBN-13: 978-1-4358-5265-5 (library binding)
1. Law—Vocational guidance—United States—Juvenile literature. 2. Criminal justice, Administration of—Vocational guidance—United States—Juvenile literature. I. Title.
KF297.O77 2009
340.023'73—dc22
                                              2008041018

Manufactured in China

CONTENTS

INTRODUCTION

O ver thirteen long months in 1976 and 1977, a serial killer nicknamed the Son of Sam had the citizens of New York City looking over their shoulders in fear. They stayed away from shadows and avoided the gaze of strangers. Young women with long hair were especially scared, as they were the killer's favorite targets. During his reign of terror, the Son of Sam shot more than a dozen people with his .44 caliber revolver. Six of those people died.

The Son of Sam was finally arrested, and when people saw him, they were surprised. This twenty-four-year-old postal clerk named David Berkowitz did not look evil. In fact, he didn't seem remotely threatening. Almost immediately, however, people questioned his mental competency to stand trial. After all, Berkowitz claimed that he had killed people based on orders coming from his neighbor's dog. Supposedly, embedded in the dog's barking were messages from a six-thousand-year-old demon that was instructing him to go out and kill young women. Despite this bizarre reasoning, psychologists ruled that the murderer was competent enough to be tried for his crimes.

In court during Berkowitz's trial, the young defendant appeared calm day after day. He was polite, and his behavior was reasonable. His round face seemed friendly, almost kind. How could someone like this possibly be one of history's most notorious serial killers? On June 23, 1978, the day of his sentencing, everyone in the courtroom learned the answer to that question.

Court had been in session for ninety minutes, everyone waiting for Berkowitz to be brought into the courtroom. Usually, he was there on time, but not that day. When he finally arrived, the defendant was completely out of control, his clothing rumpled and dirty. His eyes bulged with anger and fear. He spat cruel words at the people in the courtroom audience. The mother of one victim collapsed in tears; a victim lashed out in fury at Berkowitz but missed.

The serial killer bit and scratched the guards who tried to restrain him. At one point, he broke away and ran for the closest window. Pulitzer Prize–winning journalist and author Jimmy Breslin was at the scene. About Berkowitz, he wrote, "He was a muffin, just this lump of dough but with that electric in him, that sizzle, sizzle, sizzle. Set him off and he exploded. He took nine or ten guards, knocked them down like bowling pins, and tried to get to the window and go out. He couldn't—it was covered—but he tried. He had inhuman strength. You could see he was a dangerous man and they took him away."

It was hard for the public to believe that hiding behind this man's easy smile was one of the country's most notorious serial killers.

In the end, Berkowitz was given six life sentences, with a maximum term of 365 years. As he was dragged out of the courtroom, the families of his victims wept. At last, this dangerous killer had been taken off the streets for good. The prosecutor had proven the case, the jury had voted with confidence, and the courtroom was—like countless times throughout history—the scene of justice being served.

THE U.S. CRIMINAL JUSTICE SYSTEM AND THE COURTS

Every weekday, in sixteen thousand courtrooms across the United States, lawyers are presenting cases, judges are listening to testimony, witnesses are telling their versions of the truth while under oath, juries are making difficult decisions, verdicts are being announced, and lives are being changed. Being part of this nation's legal system can be exciting and rewarding, and it's easy to see why many young people choose a law career of some kind. No matter what role a person plays within the judicial system, it is an important and serious one.

More than two centuries ago, the Constitution of the United States laid out three branches of the government to deal with laws: the executive, the legislative, and the judicial. While the legislative branch is responsible for creating laws and the executive is responsible for putting them into force, it is the judicial branch that decides how laws should be applied and what to do when one is broken.

The guiding principle of the U.S. court system is engraved above the entrance to the Supreme Court building in Washington, D.C.: Equal justice under the law.

The Constitution also separated the courts in the United States into federal and state courts. It is the federal courts' duty to address issues that affect the country as a whole. State courts, on the other hand, primarily deal with matters within their own jurisdictions. Both the federal and state judicial systems have a pyramid structure. At the lowest level, making up the base of the pyramid, are the federal district courts and general trial courts. This is where most cases take place. Above those courts are the federal and state appellate courts. Here, cases that have already been given a verdict in a lower court are reviewed. At the top of the pyramid are the federal Supreme Court—the highest judicial body in the country—and the states' highest courts, which go by different names, depending on the state.

LADY JUSTICE

In many courtrooms and courthouses throughout America, there is a carving or image of Lady Justice. She is a tall, blindfolded lady holding a set of scales in one hand and a sword in the other. Lady Justice is a blending of several Greek goddesses that stood for justice and fairness long ago. The blindfold indicates that she is independent and impartial— she can consider both sides of an issue without bias. The scales indicate that she is weighing the

The figure of Lady Justice reminds everyone who enters the courtroom that the focus of the procedures is fairness to all.

evidence to see which is most truthful. And the sword shows that while she may be a lady, she also has the power to enforce the law.

The figure of Lady Justice symbolizes the ideals of our society's judicial system. The system exists to set things right whenever a person has been injured, victimized, or threatened, or when one's basic civil rights have been violated. It is part of the United States' great system of checks and balances. The judicial system ensures that wrong actions come with consequences. Without the justice system in place, criminals would go unpunished, victims would go unrecognized, and the concept of justice would revert to personal revenge and retaliation.

PLAYING A PART

Many people are drawn to the legal system when it comes to choosing a career. A legal profession can be a noble and honorable undertaking, and being involved in the legal system is one way for people to feel as though they are making a difference in today's world. In addition, putting criminals behind bars and protecting the innocent can be exciting.

When you think of court-related jobs, you probably think of the official judge who sits up on the bench and the prosecuting and defense

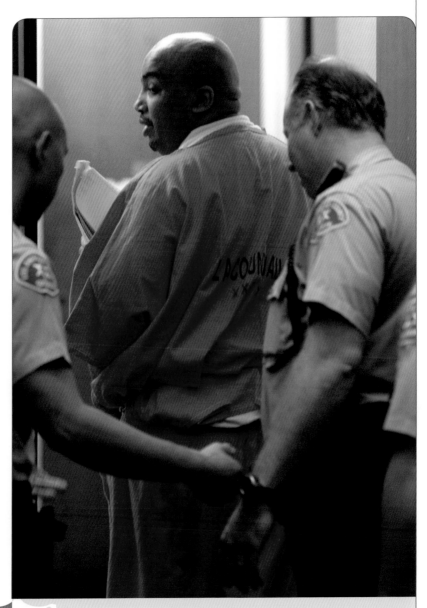

One of the key purposes of the criminal justice system is to make our society safer. These sheriff's deputies remove a convicted killer from the courtroom.

attorneys who battle back and forth to introduce evidence, cross-examine witnesses, or make closing arguments. However, there are far more people involved in the legal process than just a judge and two attorneys. A trial takes the coordination, skills, and hard work of a lot of people, and the jobs performed behind the scenes are some of the most important ones.

What jobs are available within the legal system other than those in the spotlight? Besides the judge, prosecuting attorney, and defense attorney or pro bono lawyer, here are some of the other important positions in the court arena:

- Court reporter
- Bailiff
- Interpreter
- Courtroom sketch artist
- Legal secretary
- Law clerk
- Paralegal

DRAMA ON THE SCREEN

Many young people today have grown up watching courtroom dramas unfold on television. Shows like *Law and Order* and *CSI* often focus much of their stories on trials and the process of law. You may think this trend is a recent one, but the first

Due to the popularity of the courtroom drama *Law and Order*, Angie Harmon and Sam Waterston were two of the most familiar faces on television in the late 1990s.

courtroom dramas on television actually date back to the late 1950s.

In 1957, a show called *Traffic Court* debuted on television. The cases were all based on Los Angeles traffic court trials, and the judge was UCLA law professor Edgar Allan Jones Jr. *Traffic Court* ran

Judge Joseph Wapner (*far left*) listens to plaintiffs and defendants as they explain their cases. Every afternoon for more than a dozen years, Wapner dispensed justice on *The People's Court*.

for two years and inspired a number of spin-offs, including *Day in Court, The Accused, The Verdict Is Yours,* and *Divorce Court.* During the 1960s and 1970s, interest in this type of show diminished a bit but was revived in 1981, when Ralph Edwards created *The People's Court,* with Los Angeles

Not Quite as Seen on Television

Viktor Theiss, a young assistant district attorney in Massachusetts, was interviewed by PBS for its *Frontline* program on life inside the courtroom. Theiss said he didn't think the television courtroom shows were very realistic. He said, "The entertainment value is outstanding at times, and I think some of the issues are realistic. Like *Law and Order*, they draw their material from real cases.

"The problem that they present, from my perspective and from the practical perspective, is they show easy resolution in an hour, for the most part. They don't show the long, drawn-out processes that a criminal case can be. And the arguments that they make are designed for dramatic value, not legal value. I could never make the arguments that they make on *The Practice*. My case would be instantly thrown out of court and I would have serious sanctions imposed, if I made some of the argument that they make.

"So the problem for me becomes, my jurors, who have watched these shows, there's some expectation that it's going to be like that. You know, they sit back at the trial, 'I'm going to get to watch Viktor Theiss do an opening like I just saw last night on TV.' And it's not like that."

County Superior Court judge Joseph Wapner. The original show was a huge success—it ran for 2,484 episodes during its twelve years on television.

As *The People's Court* was such a hit, other series followed, including *We the Jury* and *Moral Court*. A channel dedicated to nothing but trials and courtroom issues, called Court TV, was created in 1991. (In 2008, the channel was renamed truTV.)

The hit series *Law and Order* debuted in 1990 and continues to play in repeats and new episodes today. It is currently the longest-running prime-time drama series in the United States. Its success has resulted in several spin-offs, including *Law and Order: Special Victims Unit* and *Law and Order: Criminal Intent*.

These television shows almost certainly encourage many young people to become interested in pursuing a career in law. It is important to realize, however, that what is shown on television is a long way from reality. Real trials are not held and resolved in sixty minutes. Most cases are not full of drama and excitement every other moment as they are on television. Attorneys rarely get the chance to give long, emotional speeches to the jury as they do on many of these series. Instead, cases and trials move slowly, require a lot of unglamorous work, and often do not turn out the way everyone expected.

Despite this, a career in the U.S. legal system can be most rewarding and fulfilling. No matter what part a person plays—from legal secretary to pro bono attorney to judge—the legal system gives him or her an opportunity to make a real difference in the world. It offers the chance to uphold the ideal that every person who walks into the courtroom accused of committing a crime deserves a fair trial with knowledgeable, skilled, and dedicated people.

WORKING IN THE BACKGROUND

2

A typical courtroom often features a judge, attorneys, witnesses, defendants, juries, and an audience. Take a closer look, however, and one sees other people working away from the spotlight, each performing an important job. This chapter examines some of these creative and interesting "background" judicial system jobs. They just might have what you are looking for in a career.

RECORDING IT WORD FOR WORD: THE COURT REPORTER

Every official statement made in the courtroom, as well as in meetings and other legal conversations, has to be recorded. Not a single word can be missed. These records will be used as legal proof of what happened during the trial. Juries will study them. Attorneys will pore over them. These records must be completely accurate.

The court reporter has one of the most demanding and challenging positions within the court system. The job requires intense focus and unwavering attention.

The person responsible for making sure every word is captured is the court reporter. The job calls for speed, accuracy, and great listening skills, as well as excellent grammar, punctuation, and spelling, and a large vocabulary that includes all legal terms.

Typically, a court reporter uses a stenotype. This machine looks like an odd cross between a typewriter and a large, rather clunky adding machine. It has twenty-two keys on it, but unlike most keyboards, the keys are all blank. The keyboard is divided in two. The left side is called initial, and these are the keys used to record a word's initial consonants. The right side is called final, and it represents the final consonants of a word. Below the two sides, in the middle, are the vowels A, O, E, and U. The keys represent sounds, and several of them are pushed at the same time to create words. Even commas and periods, along with other punctuation marks, are represented by a combination of letters.

At the end of a court session, the steno paper is collected, and the symbols are translated onto a CD-ROM. Next, this is turned into normal text so that anyone can read the material. Often, the court reporter keeps medical, legal, scientific, engineering, and patent dictionaries close by to ensure that terms are spelled correctly.

In some cases, steno machines are used to do what is called real-time captioning. For this, the stenotype is directly connected to computers that translate the message so that it appears instantly on the screen for others in the courtroom to see. (You'll read more about real-time transcriptions in chapter 5.)

Learning how to use a steno machine quickly and accurately takes time, training, and practice. It is similar to learning how to read and write a foreign language. Certified court reporters can type about 220 to 225 words per minute. (The average person speaks between 160 and 180 words a minute.) Approximately three hundred post-secondary vocational and technical colleges in the United States offer some kind of court reporter training. About a third of these schools are approved by the National Court Reporters Association. It takes just under three years to earn a court reporting degree. Beyond the basic training, there are additional certifications that can be earned. These include registered professional reporter, registered merit reporter, and registered diplomate reporter. Income increases as these additional certifications are earned.

Another method used by some court reporters is voice writing. In this case, the reporter speaks directly into a stenomask, which is a handheld mask with a microphone built into it. The reporter repeats every word spoken, and it is recorded. A voice silencer ensures that no one else can hear

The Language of the Court Reporter

One look at the paper that comes out of a stenotype machine and anyone would think a big mistake had been made. The letters are scattered across the page in what looks like random order. There are no punctuation marks. There is not a single readable word on the page—unless you happen to be a stenographer. To these specially trained people, the crooked rows of letters make sense and are a clear and accurate representation of what was said that day in court. The language is largely built on shorthand, an abbreviated handwriting system that dates back thousands of years but was brought to the United States in the mid-1800s by John Robert Gregg.

In 1879, a man named Miles Bartholomew invented the stenography machine. During the 1950s, the military, along with International Business Machines Corp. (IBM), worked to create a faster and more accurate machine. By the 1970s, computer-aided transcription (CAT) was developed. CAT is used in courtrooms today.

```
T     H
                EU              S
             A        PB
     KP      A         P  L
                       P  L
                   F
       P H            PB
     S    H A         PB      D
     T P   R
          A
     ST        E    PB
            O E
       K    AO E
       PW   AO        R       D
       W
       P    A   EU   P
                E    R
               F  P L  T
```

This example of stenotype says, "This is an example of machine shorthand from a steno keyboard with paper (period)."

what is being repeated. Because this method is easier, it takes only about a year to learn.

While some court reporters work for law firms, a great many of them are freelancers. This means that they may have to travel to a different place every day. Being on call like this can be a challenge,

At this defense budget hearing, military generals testify before the U.S. Senate. A stenographer records the proceedings using a stenomask.

but for some who like flexible and spontaneous schedules, it is perfect.

The outlook for this job is fantastic—skilled court reporters are in great demand. The number of court cases in the United States is steadily growing, so the need for reliable court reporters is expected to rise. If a person likes to type, can pay a great deal of attention to detail, and has sharp listening skills, then a court reporter job may be ideal. Reporters are paid for the hours they spend at the steno machine in the courtroom, and they are also paid for each page they translate into text. (A typical six-hour steno session results in about 250 pages of text.) The job is not a difficult one physically, with the only possible problems being fatigue from sitting in the same position for hours and carpal tunnel syndrome from repetitive movements.

SAFETY FIRST: THE BAILIFF

In America, the job of protecting the people in the courtroom belongs to the bailiff. The bailiff's job begins before anyone even enters the room. He (most bailiffs are men) looks through the courtroom, checking to make sure it is clear of any weapons or bombs. He also checks to see if the room is clean and ready for use.

Once the court session begins, the bailiff really goes to work. He maintains order in the courtroom, informing everyone present of the courtroom rules and making sure all of the rules are enforced. The bailiff announces the arrival of the judge, calls witnesses to the stand, and often swears them in. He handles evidence and escorts the defendant to and from the courtroom. The bailiff is responsible for

Administering the oath to tell the truth while on the witness stand is one of the bailiff's important jobs. Lying under oath can land a witness in jail.

checking everyone who walks into the courtroom for a weapon and restraining anyone who is uncooperative or hostile. He then has the right to remove or even arrest the person. It is his job to contact medical help if necessary, or to call for additional security.

For some trials, the juries must be quarantined, or sequestered, meaning that the members cannot go back home at the end of the day. Instead, they are required to stay in a court-appointed hotel. They even have to eat at restaurants chosen by the court. When this happens, the bailiff escorts the jury members from one place to the next, and he protects them while they are sequestered. If the media or any other unauthorized people attempt to speak to jurors, then the bailiff intervenes.

The bailiff's role requires him to carry a gun. He also has to be physically fit so that he can chase someone or wrestle someone out of the room. Technically, a person is qualified for the job of bailiff if he has a high school diploma or General Educational Development (GED) credential. However, the chances of getting a job are much better for those with a degree in law enforcement or criminal justice. Some bailiffs start off as sheriff's deputies or police officers. Certain states require applicants to take the state's Peace Officers Standards and Training (POST) course, which sets selection and training standards for law enforcement officials. First-aid and self-defense skills are necessary for this job, as well as knowledge of gun safety.

TRANSLATING THE MESSAGE: THE INTERPRETER

Imagine how frightening and confusing it would be to be called to the witness stand to swear to "tell the truth, the whole truth, and nothing but the truth" in a language that was not familiar. For witnesses who do not speak English or who are hearing impaired, this is exactly what happens. Language difficulties can certainly create problems in trials, meetings, depositions, interviews, and witness preparation. This is where the court interpreter comes into the picture.

The job of the court interpreter is to relay messages to a person in a language that the person can understand. In addition to translating the literal meaning of the words, the interpreter must also be able to impart the message without any additions, omissions, or alterations to the meaning. For some, this means translating English into another language; for others, it means translating spoken language into sign language.

Naturally, a court interpreter must know at least two languages at a native or mastery level. The primary language needed for interpretation in today's

A prosecution witness testifies with the help of a courtroom interpreter during this 2003 trial in Los Angeles.

courts is Spanish, followed by Chinese, Portuguese, Vietnamese, Korean, Russian, and Arabic. Sign language interpreters are in high demand as well. They must be experts in American Sign Language (ASL), knowing the grammar rules, sentence structures, and idioms that the language uses. Interpreters who also know tactile signing—used for someone who is both deaf and blind—are in even greater demand.

Some court interpreters work in teams of two. This way, if the proceedings go on for a long time, one person can relieve the other. One also serves as backup for the other in case a term is misunderstood or needs clarification.

To prove that a person is qualified as a court interpreter, he or she is usually required to take a written examination that tests proficiency in both languages. Often, this is combined with a practical or oral exam. Currently, federal court certification for interpreters is available only in Haitian Creole, Navajo, and Spanish.

Because interpreters are hard to find, they are in great demand. Those who are certified make substantially more than those who are not. In fact, a certified interpreter will earn almost double what an uncertified one makes for the same type of work. The work environment is usually quite pleasant, and since many interpreters work freelance, they also enjoy a great deal of variety in their work.

Drawing the Image: The Sketch Artist

In 1937, cameras were banned from the courtroom. The high-profile Lindbergh baby kidnapper was on trial at the time, and every newspaper that could send a reporter did. Each day, more than seven hundred reporters and photographers tried to push their way into the courtroom. With flashbulbs popping every few seconds, it was impossible to keep order. Finally, the American Bar Association demanded changes. Cameras were forbidden in all but two states. Since then, it has been a long, slow battle to get cameras back into the courtroom. While a number of courtrooms allow them, many still do not, and none are allowed inside federal courtrooms. For these reasons, the skilled drawings of a courtroom sketch artist are essential. Without them, there would be no visual record of a trial.

Being a sketch artist at a trial requires more than just the ability to draw well. Having a formal education in art is helpful but not necessary. More important is the ability to capture people's faces and emotions. The job also requires speed and keen listening skills. The average artist tries to create five to seven drawings per day of testimony. "The deadline is so intense," said Vicki Behringer, a sketch artist. "I'm constantly looking at the clock to see how much time I have, but then something

Up Close and Personal: Sketch Artist Marilyn Church

"I've drawn the tears of victims, the pointing finger of the accuser, the despair of the condemned, and the joy of the acquitted. While other artists are drawing still lifes, landscapes, and nudes, I knew after my first day in court that I was hooked on drawing people in open warfare battling to save themselves." These are the words of well-known courtroom sketch artist Marilyn Church. She has covered some of the most sensational trials in history and has won a New York Press Club Award and an Emmy.

Her descriptions of her job definitely provide a you-are-there feeling. "The conditions are unbelievable once I've gotten a seat," she said in an interview at CourtroomArtOnline.com. "I am there now, dead center behind the defendant, balancing art supplies on my lap, jammed in on both sides by other artists, pads overlapping, all of us straining to see around guards to the defendants and hoping he'll turn his head for a moment so a profile can be caught . . . The concentration is so intense that I work on intuition, on prayer, and willing the scene to paper."

Church said she is usually too busy drawing quickly to form an opinion about a case. She often sees a side to the people in the courtroom that others miss and sometimes what she sees haunts her. "In the end, the defendant remains unknowable," she admitted. "Sometimes thoughts of them pursue me afterwards . . . I end up dreaming about them."

Courtroom artist Vicki Behringer shows her sketches from the Michael Jackson trial in 2005. Her drawings from the trial appeared in various publications and on television.

can happen that's important at the last second and you may have to include that."

Artist Marilyn Church, author of *The Art of Justice: An Eyewitness View of Thirty Infamous Trials*, wrote, "The biggest hindrance is the pressure of the deadline. I never know if a 'proceeding' will abruptly end before I'm halfway done. It's always playing 'beat the clock.'" An artist working in the courtroom has to decide which people to draw and which moments to capture. All figures have to be

immediately recognizable, too, so that when the sketches are reproduced in magazines or newspapers or are shown on television, readers and viewers will know who they are.

Church wrote, "The single most important rule I learned is that to succeed as a courtroom artist, there's never an excuse for not producing a required drawing—pens that don't work, defendants you can't see, a seat you can't get, or a face that's especially difficult to capture." Church continued, "It doesn't

This is a courtroom artist's sketch. Martha Stewart, easily recognizable at center, was on trial in 2004 for lying to federal investigators and obstructing justice.

matter how beautiful a sketch is if it doesn't make it on the air. At the end of the day I have had to remind myself that all of the tension of working at a news-making event creates an immediacy and energy that becomes part of the drawings. They are composites of many expressions and moods, communicating an entire day's events in a few images. Sometimes a good drawing can tell more than a photograph—a photograph freezes a fraction of a second, while a drawing can transcend time entirely."

Typically, sketch artists create drawings that are bought by a television station or print publication, such as a newspaper. Later, these sketches may be sold in art galleries, occasionally for thousands of dollars if the artist is known and the trial centered on celebrities like Michael Jackson or Martha Stewart. Those trials can be exceptionally challenging, and artists often have reserved seats. "There are trials where we're not allowed to leave," said artist Vicki Behringer. "Like in the Michael Jackson trial. If you leave your seat during a session, you're not allowed back into your seat until the next session. If for one reason you need to leave, to use the bathroom, you're just out of luck."

Most artists work freelance. Instead of working for a certain employer, they go to trials, draw as many sketches as possible, and then sell them to whatever media outlet offers them the most money. They carry their art supplies with them and often have to sit in a small spot in the court audience, balancing their pencils, markers, paints, or other materials on their laps. Some artists bring binoculars with them so that they can get a better view of the attorneys, witnesses, defendants, and others.

A good courtroom artist is able to express his or her artistic talent and passion for drawing while performing a much-needed and good-paying job.

As Behringer put it, "I just love drawing and love being able to stare at people and sketch their faces and expressions. I'm able to sketch them all day." Church added, "It takes a lifetime of drawing, of studying faces and gestures. It's every moment I've ever spent in a museum. It's the sum of the human experience and feelings I share with them."

3

CAREERS IN THE SPOTLIGHT

Spend a few minutes in a courtroom during a trial, and it's easy to recognize the central figures. The judge, in his or her official robe, sits high up on the bench and commands immediate attention. This person keeps close tabs on the lawyers to make sure they are following all of the rules. The other main players are the two lawyers: the prosecuting attorney and the defense attorney. The positions of judge and lawyer are crucial to the U.S. justice system. Consequently, the decision to pursue a career as a judge or lawyer cannot be made without serious consideration.

WEARING THE ROBE

The judge in a courtroom is in a position of power, control, and immense importance. As a popular superhero once stated, "With great power comes great responsibility." This is certainly true for all of the nation's judges, at

In the courtroom, the judge rules. Here, Los Angeles Superior Court judge Larry Paul Fidler sternly warns an attorney to change his behavior.

both the federal and state levels. Being a respected and trustworthy judge takes a combination of skills. You need compassion and objectivity but also the ability to listen carefully and ponder decisions slowly. Above all, you need the inner conviction that any person is innocent until proven guilty and that everyone, regardless of the crime, deserves a fair trial. This is not a job for the type of person who always has to be up and running around. It is for the person who can sit, listen, analyze, and, of course, judge.

Judges have been trained for years to preside over trials and hearings and to make sure that every trial is fair. They know how laws can and cannot be applied, and they oversee the legal process as a whole. A judge rules on the admissibility of evidence. Will it or will it not be allowed during testimony? Will it be shown to the jury? It is up to the judge to decide.

If attorneys go too far in their examinations or push the boundaries of the law, then the judge reins them in. If they start arguing over a point, then it is the judge who steps in and instructs them on how to behave—and punishes them if they do not cooperate. A judge is like a teacher in a large classroom, making sure that all rules are followed, all procedures are properly performed, and all parties are doing their jobs correctly.

Other job duties include instructing the jury on how to reach a verdict and listening to allegations and charges at pretrial hearings to decide if there is enough evidence to merit an actual trial. If there is, then the judge also determines if the person can be released on bail (and the amount) or if he or she should be kept in prison until the trial officially begins. For a bench trial, or a trial for which there is no jury, the judge alone determines the verdict of guilty or not guilty.

Of course, judges perform work outside of the courtroom, too. In their offices and in law libraries, they read documents, research judicial issues, and write opinions. They may work fifty or more hours a week.

Judges in federal courts are appointed by the president of the United States and are then confirmed by a Senate vote. For the past few decades, all of the justices appointed to serve on the U.S. Supreme Court have been federal court judges. On the state level, about half of the judges are appointed, while the other half are voted in through statewide elections.

It takes a great deal of experience to become a judge. State and federal judges typically spend years as lawyers first. The job of judge requires a person who can maintain a constant level of impartiality, has an in-depth understanding of laws, has the ability to sit patiently and listen carefully for many hours

The Face of Justice: America's Most Familiar Judge

Ask an American to think of a judge, and one person usually comes to mind: Judge Judy. That isn't too surprising considering that she has been on afternoon television dispensing advice, judgments, and lectures for more than a decade. What you may not know about Judge Judy—otherwise known as Judy Sheindlin—is that before she hit the television screen, she had built up a great deal of experience.

Sheindlin was born in Brooklyn, New York, and got her law degree from American University's School of Law in Washington, D.C. She was the only woman in her class of 126. For two years, she worked as a corporate lawyer for a cosmetics firm and then left to raise her two children. Later, she worked in family court dealing with such difficult issues as juvenile crime, domestic violence, and child abuse. In 1982, New York mayor Ed Koch appointed her as a judge in criminal court. Four years later, Sheindlin was promoted to supervising judge for the Manhattan district family court.

Sheindlin's no-nonsense attitude earned her quite a reputation. Although she retired in 1996, Sheindlin agreed to host a new courtroom show launching later that year. *Judge Judy* was a big success, and by its third year, it reached the number-one slot for syndicated shows. More than ten million people tune in to watch the show today.

JUDGE JUDY SHEINDLIN

at a time, and is able to make final, serious decisions based on hard evidence—decisions that have the potential to change, or even end, a person's life.

BECOMING AN ATTORNEY

With so many lawyers in movies, on television, and in books, it seems like most people would know what it takes to become an attorney. The job is often glamorized, however, and what is seen on television is rarely an accurate representation of what the job involves. If you love to argue or debate, then becoming a lawyer may be a great career choice. The lawyers are certainly the ones in the spotlight during a trial, so someone who doesn't feel comfortable in that position, who is shy or self-conscious, or who is simply not at his or her best in front of a crowd would be better off pursuing a different legal job.

The first step in becoming an attorney is getting a four-year college degree. While there is no official pre-law curriculum a student must take as an undergraduate, experts do recommend that prospective lawyers become proficient in certain areas. These include writing, public speaking, reading, and logical analysis. It's also a good idea to take classes in foreign languages, government, history, philosophy, political science, and computer science.

On television, attorneys spend a lot of time performing for juries in the courtroom. In real life, however, they spend more time doing research and other reading.

A Complete Human Life: Oliver Wendell Holmes Jr.

One of the most honored judges in history was Oliver Wendell Holmes Jr. Born in 1841 in Boston, Massachusetts, Holmes was the son of a well-known writer. After graduating from Harvard in 1861, he served for three years in the Civil War. During the war, he was seriously injured three times. Yet, he managed to rise to the rank of captain.

After earning his law degree in 1866, Holmes joined a law firm, where he worked for fifteen years. He taught law to other students and became the editor of the prestigious *American Law Review* magazine. In 1882, the governor appointed Holmes to the Massachusetts Supreme Court. He served there for two decades, until President Theodore Roosevelt nominated him to the U.S. Supreme Court. Amazingly, Holmes served in that position for twenty-nine years—longer than anyone before or since.

In addition to being an experienced and skillful judge, Holmes also wrote many speeches and papers. His elo-quence earned him an excellent reputation among his colleagues. He was given the nickname "the Great Dissenter" for his ability to be at odds with others while explaining himself with sound legal reasoning.

After graduation from college, students apply to law schools. Whether or not they are accepted depends on a combination of factors, including grade average, prior work experience, and their performance on the LSAT, or Law School Admissions Test. Some schools also require a personal interview with the applicant. Competition is intense, especially for the top schools, and there are always more applicants than there are openings.

If a student is accepted, then it is time for three years of law school. The better law schools are accredited by the American Bar Association, meaning that the school's faculty, library, and classes meet set standards. In 2005, there were almost ninety approved law schools throughout the United States.

The first half of law school is spent taking core courses like constitutional law, contracts and torts, and research and legal documents. Over the second half of law school, students decide which kind of law they want to specialize in. They also spend this time getting practical experience in legal clinics and taking part in mock scenarios and trials, along with researching and writing for the school's law journal.

There are several different types of lawyers. Law students may choose to go into criminal or civil law, and they may decide to be a defense attorney or a prosecutor. In addition, they may work through a law firm or in a private practice.

Defense Attorney

A defense attorney advocates for the accused, working on the important legal principle that the accused is innocent until proven guilty. The defense attorney reviews the case and seeks evidence and witnesses to corroborate the defendant's story.

Some defense attorneys are pro bono lawyers, or public defenders. As such, they provide free legal help for clients who are unable to pay for their services. (The state pays the salary of a public defender.) It is a very demanding job, with these lawyers commonly handling thirty to forty cases at a time.

Some private legal offices, too, perform pro bono work, with lawyers volunteering their time and efforts. Pro bono coordinators or managers communicate with courts and public interest organizations to help provide qualified legal services for deserving individuals or organizations. In addition, experienced coordinators often provide support and training for lawyers handling individual pro bono legal cases. For those interested in a career as a pro bono coordinator, the National Association of Pro Bono Professionals provides certification and professional development.

Prosecuting Attorney

A prosecuting attorney is responsible for presenting the case in a criminal trial against an individual suspected of breaking the law. The prosecutor is the legal representative of the jurisdiction (state, county, or district, for example) in which the alleged crime took place.

The prosecutor often visits the crime scene, reviews evidence, interviews witnesses, requests additional tests from forensics, and prepares for trial. Viktor Theiss, a prosecuting attorney in Massachusetts, described his job on *Frontline*: "It's the best job I've ever had. I love being a DA [district attorney]. At the end of the day, I get to go home and know that I accomplished something and that there are so many times during the day when I'm making these massive decisions about whether we should prosecute, if we do prosecute, what should the sentence be, and I'm working with people that, but for my efforts, would have no voice—victims of domestic violence, child victims, some of the elderly, just people in the community . . . It's a great mission to know that when you go to work, you're not just working for some kind of corporate entity, one individual's wishes—but that you have this higher principle that you act according to."

Theiss went on to impart some advice to those students considering a career as a prosecuting

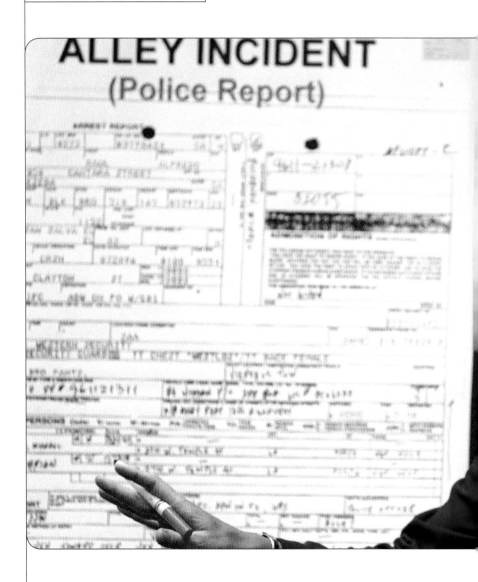

attorney: "If you really want to be a good DA, I think you have to really begin focusing on developing interpersonal skills, learning how to interact with a wide variety of people . . . You want to really study in law school some of the underlying

Prosecuting attorneys present various pieces of evidence to establish a suspect's guilt. Here, a prosecutor in a police corruption trial shows the jury a questionable police report.

procedures and the law that governs them." He added, "While you're an undergrad, taking some courses on the criminal justice system will give you a huge leg up. Understanding some of the societal factors that are involved in crime is huge . . . in general, having life experiences that take you outside what your normal role may be."

Criminal Lawyers

Whether on the prosecuting or defense side, being a criminal lawyer takes a combination of determination, commitment, knowledge, patience, and an ability to work well with a lot of people. Typically, these lawyers handle such crimes as:

- Traffic violations
- Petty theft
- Possession of drugs
- Rape
- Grand theft
- Assault and battery
- Assault with a deadly weapon
- Homicide/murder

The trials for these crimes involve many different people, so a criminal lawyer needs to be a real team player.

Civil Lawyers

Different from a criminal lawyer, a civil lawyer focuses on such legal documents as wills, trusts, contracts, titles, and leases. Civil law, as opposed

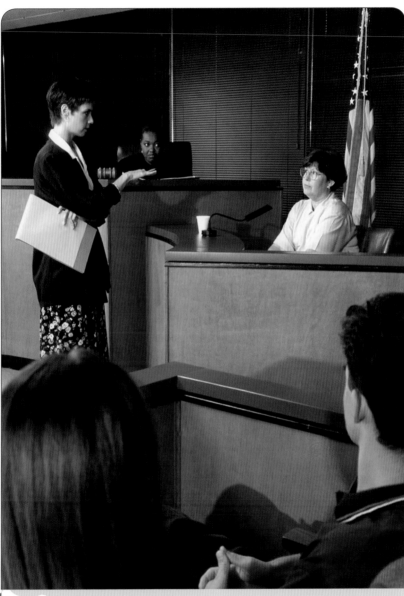

During a civil trial, attorneys often focus on the amount of compensation that victims should receive rather than on if a person is guilty or not guilty.

to criminal law, settles disputes in which money (compensation) may be awarded to the victim(s). A number of specialties are available for civil lawyers, depending on their passions and interests. These specialties include:

- Bankruptcy law
- Environmental law
- Family law
- Intellectual property law
- Probate law
- Real estate law
- Insurance law
- International law

Finally, after seven years of college, a person has a law degree—but that doesn't mean he or she is a lawyer yet. One big step still remains: passing the bar exam. This is a six-hour test that determines how much a person has learned about laws and the legal system. It is not until a person has passed a state's bar exam that he or she is an official lawyer. Some states may also have additional requirements, such as written ethics or essay exams.

In addition to being in the courtroom, some lawyers pursue careers as law professors. Others may decide to work for the federal government, investigating cases for the U.S. Department of

Justice. Most lawyers work at least forty hours a week. If they are in private practice, as seven out of ten lawyers are, they may work far more than forty hours a week. This is especially the case when they are just starting their careers.

4

CAREERS IN THE OFFICE

W hen you are watching a good movie, everything works so smoothly because of the hard work of people who never appear on-screen. Without producers, directors, cameramen, computer graphic designers, and many others, there would be no movie at all. A handful of actors and assorted props aren't enough to create a film. It is the same way in the courtroom. Lawyers and judges play key roles, but if it weren't for the help they get back in the office, the trial could not take place.

KEEPING IT ALL IN ORDER

One of the most influential positions in the entire legal system is that of legal secretary. This person is often the first one you meet when dealing with a legal firm or attorney's office. The secretary is the one who relays phone calls, delivers messages, schedules appointments, and generally makes sure that the boss is in the right place at the right time. It is no surprise that some legal secretaries are better known as information managers.

However, a legal secretary's job goes far beyond the basic clerical duties of most office secretaries. He or she handles the basic desk jobs, including filing papers, organizing paperwork, and maintaining contact with clients via phone, e-mail, and postal mail. But the legal secretary must also conduct some legal research, create spreadsheets and multimedia presentations, and provide materials requested by the attorney, paralegal, or legal assistant. A great amount of office time is spent preparing and proofreading various legal documents, such as legal invoices, deposition notices, pleadings, briefs, and subpoenas. Another big responsibility is keeping a legal or trial calendar, complete with legal filing deadlines, hearings, meetings, and closings. Deadlines in the legal system are extremely important, as filing a form one day late or forgetting to respond to one can jeopardize an entire case.

Anyone interested in the job of legal secretary should be extremely organized and know how to pay attention to detail in the midst of chaos. Fast and up-to-date computer skills are essential, as is knowing how to meet the multiple daily needs of clients and employers. Excellent spelling, grammar,

and punctuation skills are vital. Anyone can apply to be a law clerk straight out of high school. But most experts recommend that applicants learn office skills and take a one- or two-year post-high school course in legal topics. These topics would include criminal or company law, civil litigation, and other classes that teach the basics about legal terms and procedures. The National Association for Legal Professionals offers certificates to those who pass a four-hour, three-part exam, and there

Legal secretaries are multitaskers—they have no problem keeping up with several responsibilities, all at the same time.

are some online schools that also offer legal secretary certification. The job outlook for this position is good and is expected to remain so in the foreseeable future.

ORGANIZING FOR THE COURTROOM

Another clerical job that is necessary to the system is the court clerk. Court clerks have been described as the oil that keeps the court's engine running smoothly. A good court clerk is a person who can multitask, jumping from one duty to another seamlessly. Being able to process paperwork efficiently is helpful; being able to follow up on missing paperwork and other obstacles is mandatory. Clerks keep quite busy with a long list of duties. Once a case has been scheduled on the calendar, the court clerk sends a letter to those participating in the process, announcing when and where the trial will be held. Next, the clerk prepares a folder for the case and then, over time, adds relevant documents to it.

After a legal document is submitted to the court, the clerk is responsible for checking it for accuracy. If there is a mistake, then the clerk goes back to the person who completed the form and explains the problem. Just before a case begins, the clerk checks the case folder to make sure that all of the pertinent paperwork is enclosed. If something is missing, then the clerk has to track it down.

In addition to helping lawyers, court clerks also assist judges by contacting witnesses and preparing any forms that the judge might need during a hearing or trial. When a case is under way in the courtroom, it is often the court clerk who swears in the jurors and witnesses. Court clerks also keep track of case results, court orders, and unpaid fees. They collect court fees or fines, as well as bail payments, and they make sure that the amount is recorded properly. Typically, clerks are also responsible for filing public records, such as mortgages, deeds, and marriage licenses. A court clerk is often given the responsibility of maintaining custody of trial evidence and numbering and labeling it for identification.

You can become a court clerk with a high school diploma or certificate of General Educational Development (GED). However, your chances of landing a job are better if you also have at least two years of college or business school. A bachelor's degree is helpful. To be a federal court clerk, you are expected to have a master's degree or law degree. Clearly, all English language skills must be excellent, as well as familiarity with word processing, bookkeeping, accounting, and business management.

LAW CLERK

Law clerks, who are usually attorneys, work closely with a judge to help him or her make informed legal decisions. They help in courtroom proceedings through their various interactions with the court's staff, the litigants, and the general public. The law clerk helps the judge review briefs, verify legal authority, perform legal research, and write various legal documents. Law clerks in

Law clerks come in all stripes. With the help of assistive technology, this federal law clerk gets the job done at the U.S. Office of Personnel Management.

appellate courts focus on research and the legal issues involved in appeals. In addition, before the proceedings begin, law clerks inform the judge and the judge's staff about the highlights of a case. This position is an influential one because a judge's decision may be guided by a clerk's recommendations.

Most law clerks are recent law school graduates who take a one- or two-year clerkship with a

judge. Usually, only the students with the highest grades are chosen for clerkships because there are only a few select openings. Anyone pursuing this position should have excellent communication skills, strong research skills, and a very thorough understanding of all aspects of court procedures, legal rules, and the court system. Unlike trial attorneys, law clerks do not have to stand up in court, although they still do research, make decisions,

Equal Opportunity: Myra Bradwell

Prior to the U.S. Civil War (1861–1865), women were not allowed to vote, own property, get divorced, or sue someone in court. After the war, a movement grew to get women more involved in society—and in law. Colleges and law schools began accepting women.

Finally, in 1869, Myra Bradwell passed the Illinois bar with honors. When she applied to her state's supreme court, however, she was rejected for being a woman. The court claimed, "The civil law, as well as nature itself, has always recognized a wide difference in the respective spheres and destinies of man and woman. Man is, or should be, woman's protector and defender. The natural and proper timidity and delicacy which belongs to the female sex evidently unfits it for many of the occupations of civil life . . ."

Fortunately, in 1890, Illinois' rules changed, and Bradwell was allowed to become a licensed attorney. When Bradwell died, her obituary noted, "The future historian will accord [Bradwell] the breaking of the chain that bound woman to a life of household drudgery. She opened the door of the professions to her sex, and compelled law makers and judges as well, to proclaim that it was not a crime to be born a woman."

and are completely involved in the judicial process. Federal law clerks make a higher annual salary than state law clerks.

PARALEGAL

Paralegal is one of the most sought-after jobs within the legal system. Without a reliable and skilled paralegal, lawyers would be in big trouble. The American Bar Association defines a paralegal as "a person qualified by education, training or work experience who is employed or retained by a lawyer, law office, corporation, governmental agency or other entity who performs specifically delegated substantive legal work for which a lawyer is responsible."

The list of what paralegals can do for a lawyer is extensive. In fact, it is easier to list what they cannot do: paralegals are not allowed to set legal fees, give anyone legal advice, or present a case in the courtroom. Otherwise, if it happens in a lawyer's office, then paralegals are probably authorized to do it.

Paralegals help lawyers prepare for all kinds of proceedings, from hearings and trials to closings and corporate meetings. They investigate many of the facts in a case and gather all of the most relevant information. They then organize and analyze it. Finally, they turn their findings over to a

lawyer to study. Paralegals prepare legal arguments, write draft pleadings and motions that will be filed in court, obtain affidavits, and track all files so that they will be accessible the moment an attorney needs them. Their jobs do not end there, however. They draft legal documents, including contracts, separation agreements, and trusts, and they assist in preparing tax returns or in planning estates.

This paralegal (*right*) has the responsibility of bringing documents to and from the courtroom. The huge amount of documents needed for this case requires a cart!

Most paralegals work in law firms, in corporate legal departments, or for government offices. They often specialize in a specific area, such as:

- Litigation
- Personal injury
- Corporate law
- Criminal law

- Employee benefits
- Intellectual property
- Labor law
- Bankruptcy
- Immigration
- Real estate
- Family law

A paralegal may be able to find work with a two-year associate's degree, but it is more advantageous to have a four-year bachelor's degree. In addition to earning a secondary degree, paralegals need to go to one of the one thousand schools across the country that offer paralegal training. At least 260 of those schools are officially approved by the American Bar Association. Graduation from one of these will greatly increase the chance of getting hired.

5

IN THE WORKS

ollowing the same trend that is seen in nearly all work settings today, the traditional courtroom is quickly becoming the new and improved electronic courtroom. Technological developments and courtroom upgrades are improving the speed and efficiency of legal proceedings across the United States. For those planning to take on careers within the legal system, it's a good idea to stay on top of these developments.

Judge Roger G. Strand from Arizona likes the changes that he sees in his courtroom. "It is important that we all embrace these new technologies," Strand says, "because they truly can enable us to do our jobs in a more effective and efficient manner for the litigants who bring cases to the court system and for the public generally." Judge Edward Prado of Texas agrees. "Technology is great and it works," he says. "I would say 85 to 90 percent of the time, it does improve the presentation in the

courtroom . . . It spoils you. Now that I have it, I can't imagine going back to the old way."

DIGITAL EVIDENCE PRESENTATION SYSTEM (DEPS)

Installing a digital evidence presentation system (DEPS) in a courtroom helps speed up procedures

This forward-looking courtroom uses the latest in computer technology. Each desktop features its own video monitor so that all participants can view evidence and other relevant information at the same time.

and cut down on paperwork and waste. This system allows judges and lawyers to show evidence and other case documents to jurors on a set of large flat-screen monitors that are mounted throughout the courtroom, including in the jury box, witness box, judge's bench, courtroom reporter station, courtroom deputy station, and at counsel tables. When the evidence or document is displayed on the screens, an attorney or a witness can use an illustrator or annotation pen to highlight a small detail or unusual marking.

The DEPS is designed so that all exhibits are easy to see. It can display almost any type of courtroom evidence, including documents, three-dimensional objects, photographs, X-rays, negatives, slideshow and PowerPoint presentations, charts and graphs, and transparencies. While most of these images can be seen by the courtroom audience as well, the judge has a "kill switch" at the bench to immediately blank out certain screens if necessary. Judge Catherine Perry of Missouri explains, "The judge is always in control of the trial just like before. I realized all I needed was that one switch that turns off the jury monitors . . . I can still decide whether evidence is more prejudicial than probative. And I can control how many photographs get shown if we have an accident scene or injury site . . . My job as a judge has not changed. I still control what the jury sees and how much they see of it."

The DEPS is considered the control center. It is typically built inside a console known as a media cart. The DEPS usually includes a document camera and a touch-screen monitor so that lawyers can easily incorporate changing screens into their speeches or examination questions. The system is also designed so that laptops can be plugged into it. Chief Judge Rodney Webb of North Dakota says this new technology is really helping the court

The Courtroom of the 21st Century

Inside the William and Mary Law School's McGlothlin Courtroom in Williamsburg, Virginia, is the most technologically advanced courtroom in the United States. Known as the Courtroom 21 Project, it was founded in 1993. Its purpose is to provide judges, court reporters, law professors, attorneys, and other courtroom staff with a demonstration site to show off new, commercially available technology designed to enhance the courtroom. "We drop a metaphorical pebble in the center of the courtroom well and ripple out to all other parts of the legal system," says professor Fred Lederer, the project's director.

They experiment with the latest inventions to see just how they will help—or hinder—the legal system and the people involved in it. The project does all of this through single-subject experiments, ongoing courtroom use, and experimental laboratory trials. In addition to all of this, the Courtroom 21 Project performs ongoing legal research to keep pace with the latest technology that is being developed.

The Courtroom 21 Project conducts frequent demonstrations in Virginia and through video-teleconferencing. People working with the project also help to install the equipment and train the legal professionals who will be using it.

During this mock trial in Courtroom 21, computer technology and the Internet are used to connect witnesses, lawyers, a judge, and a jury.

save time. "In the past, in trials with a lot of papers or trials that had a lot of pictures," he says, "you had to publish these things and distribute them to the jury. Now, we publish all pictures and written documents received in evidence through the monitors, and it saves enormous amounts of time." Judge James Gwin from Ohio also appreciates the amount of time that is saved using the DEPS. "In most cases, I estimate that it moves things along 30 percent faster," he states. "In a traditional trial, there is so much dead time with lawyers shuffling

papers for witnesses' examination. Even when exhibit books are used, there's time taken to get the witness to the right pages, the right paragraph." The DEPS also includes a high-quality DVD player with freeze-frame capability so that the court can see recordings frame by frame.

VIDEO-TELECONFERENCING

One key technological change that has taken place relatively recently is the ability to regularly do video-teleconferencing in the courtroom. This technology uses video to allow witnesses who are off-site to give "live" testimony during a trial. Video-teleconferencing saves time and money because witnesses do not have to travel from far-away locations in order to testify in a courtroom.

Chief bankruptcy judge Lee Jackwig from Iowa finds video-teleconferencing quite helpful. She describes how when she is listening to testimony from the witness stand, she typically can see only the back of the speaker's head or a profile. "But a witness testifying [by video conference] is pretty much facing me on the screen," she explains. "I have a very good view of that individual and can watch the facial expression, mannerism, etc., that go into judging credibility."

Legal scholar and U.S. Court of Appeals judge Guido Calabresi was very reluctant to use this new technology. "I am one of those antediluvian people who still do everything in old-fashioned ways," he admits. "I don't use a computer . . . so when I heard about that video-conferencing, I wouldn't say I was sure it wouldn't work, but I was very skeptical." However, after using it a short time, Judge Calabresi changed his mind. "It worked out very well. I've had no problems with it at all," he says. "And more than that, I had a sense that people have been able to make their arguments in a way that is more relaxed than if they had to come rushing down from a long distance."

In addition, advanced audio equipment, like audio enhancement and infrared headphones, has been added to the courtroom to help those who are hearing impaired. Such technology also makes it easier for everyone in the courtroom to hear hard-to-understand audio evidence, such as undercover tapes.

Computer-Assisted Real-Time Transcription (CART)

One of the biggest recent advances in courtroom procedure is the development of real-time transcriptions. For these, the court reporter uses the stenographer machine as usual to record everything that is said. But, instead of the transcript being translated later, the information is immediately converted to text that can be seen on computer monitors or television or projection screens. Court reporter Ed Hawkins from the Washington, D.C., district says, "Real-time combines writing, translating, and editing into a single function."

Computer-assisted real-time transcription, or CART, was originally designed to help those with hearing impairments. It has since expanded. Now,

it is used with jurors, plaintiffs, defendants, and attorneys in conferences, meetings, and trials. By seeing what was said only seconds after it was said, attorneys can mark the places they might want to return to during later questioning or closing

As courtrooms become more heavily reliant on technology, people with computer expertise will be needed more and more.

procedures. All they have to do is press the space bar on their laptops, and the system inserts a reference mark. At the end of the day, attorneys can also go home with a rough draft of everything that was said, rather than waiting a few hours or a day. This helps them prepare for the next day's court session, thus improving efficiency.

Since real-time transcriptions can be safely sent across the Internet, experts can monitor testimony as it is being given, no matter their location. This way, they can write down questions or responses for later discussion. Judges also find advantages to real-time transcriptions. They have an instant copy to help them deal with difficult motions and rulings, they can better understand witnesses who might have a speech impediment or strong accent, and they can better review a question to a witness and then rule on a lawyer's objection to it. Judge James Robertson from the U.S. District Court for the District of Columbia says that CART helps him focus more on the trial. "The need to take notes is not as important," he points out.

Another reason that the electronic courtroom is growing in popularity is simple: with today's juries, the electronic medium is often the best way to communicate. For example, many young jury members are used to getting the majority of their news, information, and entertainment via the Internet. Those accustomed to the Net's colorful graphics, bullet lists, and brief sound bites may actually struggle to remain focused when faced with nothing but two attorneys and their note cards. Such jury members may find themselves daydreaming instead of concentrating—something that could certainly turn the course of a trial when it comes to reaching a verdict. As Judge Ben Tennille from the North Carolina Business Court puts it, "We get most of our information off of a screen these days, whether it's a computer screen, a television screen, or an iPhone screen. That's the way jurors want their information."

Although CART is helpful, not all court reporters know how to use it and not all judges will allow it in their courtrooms. Daryl Teshima, an attorney, writes, "Real-time requires a court reporter that can instantly turn a cacophony of voices into coherent, mistake-free text. There is no opportunity for the reporter to review a tape of the proceedings or clean up the rough transcript. If the court reporter is not up to speed, the ensuing transcript will probably be useless." While CART is not necessarily for everyone, for others, it is ideal. "Real-time reporting works because it represents the best of two worlds: the skill and experience of a court reporter with the speed and power of computers," writes Teshima.

Of course, all of this technology comes with a few inevitable challenges. First, courtrooms have to be rewired and updated in order to support the new and expensive equipment. Second, people have to be hired and brought in to ensure that the machines are connected correctly, maintained properly, and repaired quickly. Third, judges and attorneys have to be trained to use the equipment, which can take some time. Some attorneys struggle to use the DEPS because they are used to being the center of attention when presenting important evidence. With the new technology, however, juries and others in the courtroom tend to stare at the screen instead of the lawyer. Finally, there are going to be unavoidable glitches with the equipment. Attorneys must have a plan B in place in case their PowerPoint presentation or their slideshow suddenly is unusable.

IN THE FUTURE

s there such a thing as pre-law for a student who wants to pursue a career in the legal system? Is there a set curriculum that students should follow in order to prepare for a career in the courtroom or on the legal sidelines? Actually, no—there isn't any such program at this point. Majoring in one field over another is not likely to make any significant difference in whether or not a student gets accepted into law school. Instead, the American Bar Association recommends that students focus on whatever area of study they find the most fascinating and challenging. As one law school phrases it, "Whatever you pursue as an undergraduate, from liberal arts to business, from engineering to social science, from chemistry to physical education, from education to journalism, you will be eligible for law school. This means that it is never too late to choose law as a career."

The Web site for the College of Charleston warns pre-law students that "a narrowly based,

unchallenging major with vocational objectives is not the best preparation. A student should seek out a challenging, quality education. Law schools want students who can think analytically, read critically, and write intelligently and correctly. Any course of

Law students pass many, many hours in their university's legal libraries. This time is spent studying, researching, doing homework, and talking to fellow classmates about legal issues.

study that helps develop critical analyses, logical reasoning, written expression, computer skills, and oral facility is recommended." The Web site continues, "Whatever your major turns out to be, you must make good grades. However, excellent grades in unchallenging courses are false steps. Finally, remember that law school is mostly reading, research, and writing. If you do not enjoy those exercises, do not go to law school."

Many undergraduate schools have pre-law advisers who give students guidance on what core skills they need to develop. Most commonly, these skills include:

- Analytic/problem-solving skills
- Critical reading
- Writing skills, especially persuasive writing
- Oral communication/listening abilities
- General research skills with computers, books, and interviews
- Task organization/management skills
- Public service and promotion of justice
- Vocabulary acquisition
- Familiarity with libraries and resources

In addition, experts also recommend that students develop:

- Wide understanding of American history, including how society, politics, economics, and the culture have affected it
- Fundamental comprehension of political thought and the U.S. political system

(continued)

Who Wins?

A film producer is found dead in his Hollywood home. Everyone's eyes are on the actress who had just fought with him. Was the antique gun found at the scene the murder weapon? Was it all done out of revenge?

For three Napa Valley high school students, those were important questions that they had to answer. The one who did the best at this mock trial would go on to compete on the state level with students from almost forty other schools. Students were given roles from judge and attorneys to witnesses and jury members. Some students were clearly interested in pursuing a career in the law, while others were just there to learn something interesting and have a good time.

The mock trial calls for various skills, including quick thinking, poise, self-confidence, and improvisation. "There is no end to the benefits of this activity," says Napa High teacher and adviser Eileen Guerard. "Students have to know details and 'big-picture' questions, think on their feet and respond to changing trial environments, speak clearly and intelligently and, ultimately, impress the adults who will be judging them." She adds, "Every year without fail, the judges who volunteer to adjudicate the county competition remark that they wish every lawyer who presents a case in front of them would be as prepared as our students are."

- Basic awareness of math and financial skills
- Concepts related to human behavior and social interaction
- Familiarity with diverse cultures within and beyond the United States, as well as knowledge of world events and the inter-dependence of this nation with others

A high school student participates in a mock trial inside senate chambers in Austin, Texas. The annual event is organized by YMCA Texas Youth and Government.

Finding Information and Getting Experience

Reading a book about careers in the courts is great. But to get a better idea of whether a job in the legal system is the right career path, students

The students pictured on the Monroe College Web site (http://www.monroecollege.edu) participated in Monroe's Summer Law Program.

should find a way to experience it and learn about it up close. There are several ways to do this.

Several colleges across the United States offer summer law camps and workshops. For example, Monroe College in New York offers a weeklong

APPLY NOW CONTACT US REQUEST INFO

GO

Prospective Students | Alumni | Employers | Parents

Monroe

Print this page

nroe / News / Archives / News From 2007 / Summer Law Program (8/24/2007)

Weekly Observer

Weekly Observer
Read about Monroe's latest news and happenings.

Submit material to:
Weekly Observer Editor

Monroe Observer

Monroe Observer
Published three times each year, the Monroe Observer provides a summary of recent college events.

My Monroe

My MONROE
● Customize It!
● Personalize It!
● Experience It!

Login Page

gram

cipated in Monroe College's Summer Law Program will
show for their summer vacation than photographs and
resume their high school studies in September.

about the three credits I was going to receive," said
, 17, a senior at Hempstead High school in Long Island.
he program got underway, I realized that I had begun a
towards making decisions about my future."

h school students participated in a college-level, three-
e New Rochelle campus that included interactive lectures
h seasoned criminal justice professionals. Additionally,
to forensics and ballistics labs, police departments.

summer law program. Classes include Introduction to the American Legal Systems, Criminal Law, and Civil Rights Law. The program offers high school students a chance to meet face to face with practicing lawyers and judges or to participate in an actual search-and-seizure suppression hearing. On the opposite coast, the UCLA School of Law sponsors a weeklong program called the Summer Law Institute. It offers students an opportunity to interact with attorneys, visit law offices, study under law professors, and even go out to lunch with a judge.

The Michigan Supreme Court Learning Center offers programs for junior high and high school students. Rachael Drenovsky, coordinator of the program, says high school students "will practice skills that they would need in the law, while the junior high group will observe actual court proceedings." The goal of the program is to give the students a real-life view of legal careers.

Students may also want to contact their state's bar association to see if the state offers summer classes, courtroom tours, or other services. Many states do—and even if they don't, enough requests may just inspire them to create some.

Finally, to uncover other opportunities to learn more about the legal system, students can talk to their school guidance or career counselors. They may know about local programs that allow students to shadow, or observe, a professional in the criminal justice system as he or she goes about the job. Career counselors may also know of mentoring possibilities or law office internships. There are opportunities in almost every community for students to pursue.

Careers in law attract many students who want to make a difference in the world. Others want the respect and attention that the job can bring. Still others like the sheer excitement that the profession can generate. As a high school mock trial contestant puts it, "It's that feeling you get when you're in the courtroom, up on the stand, the whole unpredictability of it. It's the thrill and euphoric feeling you get."

GLOSSARY

affidavit Sworn statement.

antediluvian Ancient; made or developed a long time ago.

bailiff Court official charged with securing the courtroom.

battery Act of battering or beating.

captioning Converting to written word or translating.

cross-examine To ask questions of a witness in order to check or discredit his or her previous testimony.

deposition Witness's testimony.

dissenter In a legal sense, one who disagrees with a majority decision.

euphoric Elated; feeling exceptionally well.

forensics Application of science to legal problems.

idioms Expressions in the usage of language that have a peculiar or nonstandard meaning.

impartial Fair, unbiased, or without prejudice.

judge Senior official in a court of law.

jurisdiction Area of legal authority.

legal secretary Person who does clerical duties in a law firm or private practice.

litigant Person or party involved in a lawsuit.

paralegal Lawyer's assistant.

pro bono Describing legal work done for no cost.

proficiency Thorough skillfulness.

prosecuting attorney Lawyer charged with showing why a defendant is guilty.

quarantine To force into isolation.

resolution Point in a drama at which the conflict is worked out.

sequester To isolate or set apart from others.

stenomask Handheld recording mask used by court reporters.

stenotype Recording instrument used by court reporters.

tactile signing Sign language for those who are both visually and hearing impaired.

testimony Evidence given in court.

torts Legal classification of wrongful acts.

verdict Official court judgment.

vocational Relating to a job or career skills.

FOR MORE INFORMATION

American Bar Association (ABA)
321 N. Clark Street
Chicago, IL 60654-7598
(800) 285-2221
Web site: http://www.abanet.org
The ABA provides law school accreditation, continuing legal education, information about the law, programs to assist lawyers and judges in their work, and initiatives to improve the legal system for the public.

**National Association for
    Court Management (NACM)**
300 Newport Avenue
Williamsburg, VA 23185-4147
(757) 259-1841
Web site: http://www.nacmnet.org
The NACM is devoted to addressing court management issues in federal, state, and local courts.

**National Association of Freelance
    Legal Professionals (NAFLP)**
9930 Mesa Rim Road #1600
San Diego, CA 92121

Web site: http://www.freelancelegalprofessionals.
blogspot.com
The NAFLP is a nationwide community of freelance
attorneys, paralegals, court reporters, interpreters, and
other freelance legal professionals.

National Association of Judiciary Interpreters
and Translators (NAJIT)
603 Stewart Street, Suite 610
Seattle, WA 98101
(202) 293-0342
Web site: http://www.najit.org
The NAJIT is a professional association that promotes
quality services in the field of legal interpreting and
translating.

National Association of Legal Assistants (NALA)
1516 S. Boston #200
Tulsa, OK 74119
(918) 587-6828
Web site: http://www.nala.org
The NALA provides continuing education and
professional development programs for legal assistants
and paralegals.

National Association for Legal Professionals (NALS)
8159 East 41st Street
Tulsa, OK 74145
(918) 582-5188

Web site: http://www.nals.org
The NALS offers professional development by providing continuing legal education, certifications, information, and training to those in the legal services industry.

National Association of Women Lawyers (NAWL)
American Bar Center
321 N. Clark Street, 15th Floor
Chicago, IL 60654
(312) 988-6186
Web site: http://www.nawl.org
The NAWL is a national voluntary legal professional organization devoted to promoting the interests and progress of women lawyers and women's legal rights.

National Court Reporters Association (NCRA)
8224 Old Courthouse Road
Vienna, VA 22182
(800) 272-6272
Web site: http://www.ncraonline.org
The NCRA establishes ethical standards, performs testing and certification, conducts research and analysis, and offers educational opportunities for professional court reporters.

Registry of Interpreters for the Deaf (RID)
333 Commerce Street
Alexandria, VA 22314
(703) 838-0030

Web site: http://www.rid.org
The RID is a national membership organization representing the professionals who facilitate communication between people who are deaf or hard of hearing and people who can hear. Interpreters serve as professional communicators in a vast array of settings, including courtrooms.

U.S. Court Reporters Association (USCRA)
P.O. Box 465
Chicago, IL 60690-0465
(800) 628-2730
Web site: http://www.uscra.org
The USCRA is the national representative for the federal court reporting profession.

Web Sites

Due to the changing nature of Internet links, Rosen Publishing has developed an online list of Web sites related to the subject of this book. This site is updated regularly. Please use this link to access the list:

http://www.rosenlinks.com/ccj/cour

FOR FURTHER READING

Baum, Lawrence. *The Supreme Court*. Washington, DC: Congressional Quarterly Press, 2006.

Bell-Rehwoldt, Sheri. *Careers for the Twenty-First Century: Law*. Farmington Hills, MI: Lucent Books, 2004.

Camenson, Blythe. *Careers for Legal Eagles and Other Law-and-Order Types*. New York, NY: McGraw-Hill Books, 2005.

Field, Shelly. *Ferguson Career Coach: Managing Your Career in Law Enforcement*. New York, NY: Ferguson Publishing Company, 2008.

Friedman, Jane M. *America's First Woman Lawyer: The Biography of Myra Bradwell*. Amherst, NY: Prometheus Books, 1993.

Grippando, James. *Leapholes*. Chicago, IL: American Bar Association, 2006.

Hiber, Amanda. *Should Cameras Be Allowed in Courtrooms?* Farmington Hills, MI: Greenhaven Press, 2008.

Koss, Amy Goldman. *Poison Ivy*. New York, NY: Roaring Brook Press, 2006.

Margulies, Philip. *The Devil on Trial: Witches, Anarchists, Atheists, Communists and Terrorists*

in America's Courtrooms. Boston, MA:
Houghton-Mifflin Books, 2008.
Reeves, Diane Lindsey. *Career Ideas for Teens in Law and Public Safety*. New York, NY:
Checkmark Books, 2006.
Weatherford, Carole Boston. *Great African American Lawyers: Raising the Bar of Freedom*. Berkeley Heights, NJ: Enslow Publishers, 2003.

BIBLIOGRAPHY

Administrative Office of the U.S. Courts. "Courtroom Technology Used Increasingly to Enhance Proceedings." *The Third Branch*, Vol. 35, No. 5, May 2003. Retrieved August 22, 2008 (http://www.uscourts.gov/ttb/may03ttb/technology.html).

Administrative Office of the U.S. Courts. "Realtime Court Reporting Grows in Popularity." *The Third Branch*, Vol. 37, No. 12, December 2005. Retrieved August 22, 2008 (http://www.uscourts.gov/ttb/dec05ttb/realtime/index.html).

Anderson, James F., Nancie Mangels, and Laronistine Dyson. *Criminal Justice and Criminology: A Career Guide to Local, State, Federal and Academic Positions*. Lanham, MD, University Press of America, 2003.

Arlington National Cemetery. "Oliver Wendell Holmes Jr." Retrieved August 19, 2008 (http://www.arlingtoncemetery.net/owholmes.htm).

Camenson, Blythe. *Careers for Legal Eagles and Other Law-and-Order Types*. New York, NY: McGraw-Hill Books, 2005.

Church, Marilyn, and Lou Young. *The Art of Justice: An Eyewitness View of Thirty Infamous Trials*. Philadelphia, PA: Quirk Books, 2006.

Connor, Tracy. "When He Held the City in Fear." NYDailyNews.com, June 3, 2007. Retrieved August 22, 2008 (http://www.nydailynews.com/news/ny_crime/2007/06/03/2007-06-03_when_he_held_the_city_in_fear.html).

Echaore-McDavid, Susan. *Career Opportunities in Law Enforcement, Security and Protective Services*. New York, NY: Checkmark Books, 2006.

Flythe, Tammi. "The Courtroom 21 Project: A Light at the End of the Legal Technology Tunnel." The Courtroom Information Project. Retrieved August 22, 2008 (http://technology.findlaw.com/articles/01057/009999.html).

Jones, Jillian. "Students Try on Legal Profession at Mock Trial Competition." NapaValleyRegister.com, March 1, 2008 (http://www.napavalleyregister.com/articles/2008/03/01/news/local/doc47c9000444873401612316.txt).

Lambert, Stephen, and Debra Regan. *Great Jobs for Criminal Justice Majors*. New York, NY: McGraw-Hill Books, 2007.

Michigan Supreme Court, Office of Public Information. March 17, 2006. Retrieved

September 15, 2008 (http://courts.michigan.
gov/SUPREMECOURT/Press/
LearningCenterCareers.pdf).

Monroe College. "Prospective Students." Retrieved
August 18, 2008 (http://www.monroecollege.
edu/prospectivestudents/highschoolstudents/
summerlawprogram/programcontent).

Morgan, Marilyn. *Careers in Criminology.* New
York, NY: McGraw-Hill Books, 2000.

PageWise, Inc. "Myra Bradwell: America's First
Woman Lawyer." Essortment.com, 2002.
Retrieved August 22, 2008 (http://www.
essortment.com/all/myrabradwell_rfxv.htm).

PBS.org. "Interview: Prosecutor Viktor Theiss."
November 2000. Retrieved August 18, 2008
(http://www.pbs.org/wgbh/pages/frontline/
shows/bostonda/etc/theiss.html).

Phillips, Jennifer. "Hot Trials Raise Profile of
Sketch Artists." Columbia University. Retrieved
August 20, 2008 (http://jscms.jrn.columbia.edu/
cns/2006-03-14/phillips-courtroomsketch).

PrelawHandbook.com. "Advice for a Pre-Law
Student Selecting an Undergraduate Major."
Retrieved August 24, 2008 (http://www.
prelawhandbook.com/prelaw_and_major).

Rash, Michelle Cater. "Tech on Trial: State-of-the-Art
Technology Playing a Bigger Role in Courtrooms."
The Business Journal, August 22, 2008. Retrieved

August 24, 2008 (http://www.bizjournals.com/
triad/stories/2008/08/25/focus1.html).

SoYouWanna.com. "SoYouWanna Be a
Paralegal?" Retrieved August 17, 2008 (http://
www.soyouwanna.com/site/syws/paralegal/
paralegal.html).

Stinchcomb, James. *Opportunities in Law
Enforcement and Criminal Justice Careers.*
New York, NY: McGraw-Hill Books, 2003.

Teshima, Daryl. "Realtime Transcription Offers
Real-World Advantages." *Los Angeles Lawyer
Magazine*, 2000. Retrieved August 29, 2008
(http://www.lacba.org/lalawyer/tech/
comp3-00.html).

TV.com. "Judge Judy Sheindlin." Retrieved
August 22, 2008 (http://www.tv.com/
judge-judy-sheindlin/person/422220/
biography.html).

INDEX

ABOUT THE AUTHOR

Tamra Orr is an award-winning author of more than 150 nonfiction books for readers of all ages. She and her husband live in the Pacific Northwest.

PHOTO CREDITS

Cover (background images) © www.istockphoto.com/Lisa F. Young, © www.istockphoto.com/David Lewis; cover (inset silhouette), p. 1 © www.istockphoto.com/Jaroslaw Wojcik; pp. 6, 29, 32, 72–73, 76–77, 86–87 © AP Images; p. 9 Alex Wong/Getty Images; pp. 11, 48 Library of Congress Prints and Photographs Division; p. 13 Genaro Molina–Pool/Getty Images; p. 15 © NBC/courtesy Everett Collection; pp. 16–17 © Warner Brothers/courtesy Everett Collection; p. 22 Jupiter Images/Newscom; p. 25 Wikipedia.org; pp. 26–27 Mark Wilson/Getty Images; pp. 36–37 Stan Honda/AFP/Getty Images; p. 38 Jane Rosenberg/Getty Images; p. 42 Jamie Rector/Getty Images; p. 45 Getty Images; p. 47 Scott T. Baxter/Photodisc/Getty Images; pp. 52–53 Lucy Nicholson/AFP/Getty Images; p. 55 © Bob Daemmrich/The Image Works; pp. 60–61 krtphotoslive/Newscom; pp. 64–65 Scott J. Ferrell/Congressional Quarterly/Getty Images; p. 66 Archive Photos/Hulton Archive/ Getty Images; pp. 68–69 James Nielsen/AFP/Getty Images; pp. 80–81 Adrin Snider–Pool/Getty Images; pp. 90–91 © Bob Daemmrich/PhotoEdit; pp. 92–93 Used with permission, Summer Law Program, Monroe College.

Designer: Les Kanturek; Editor: Christopher Roberts

WHEELER HS/MS MEDIA CENTER
NORTH STONINGTON, CT 06359
860-535-0377